10 Tips to Amazon Arbitrage Success

Garry Ray

DEDICATION

This book is dedicated to my beautiful wife, Kimberly Jordan Ray
.

CONTENTS

RECOMMENDATIONS

"Garry speaks from the heart. He evaluates his success by the success of those he is coaching. High standards and high expectations"
Dan Wentworth, Multiple 7 Figure Seller

"I learn something valuable from Garry every time I hear him speak. Decades of business success and life learning enable him to share wisdom profitable to any entrepreneur."
Nathan Slamans, Co-Founder, Amazing Freedom

"You can't stop a giver from giving. Garry Ray is that giver."
Gaye Lisby, Founder, Amazon Seller Tribe, 7 Figure Seller

"Garry is an outstanding professional, an expert in business and life. His expertise about selling on Amazon is creative, insightful and right. He is highly motivated and driven by an amazing passion to succeed. Garry embodies a perfect mix of the attributes I look for in a mentor: personal impact, great analytics and excellent problem solving skills. He couples this with his insatiable interest in serving Amazon sellers."
Andy Slamans, Multiple 7 Figure Seller and Private Label Leader, Co-Founder, Amazing Freedom

Prologue

What good is making money or being successful if you don't take time to share some of it? I believe we should try to help new people. What I share here might not help very many veteran Amazon sellers.

If you've been in this business a long time, you'll get a little bit out of it, but the people who could really be helped are new third party sellers who feature arbitrage as their business model.

But first, let me tell you a little about my Amazon journey and how I came to be here.

I'm an average guy, from an average place, made average grades in school. Nothing special about me at all. Rocked in the gospel cradle but raised around people who were negative about money and succeeding with their finances.

I'm nothing special other than I always had a strong desire to succeed. I had a man who took interest in training me in the insurance industry when I was 18 ½ years old.

Although I was surrounded by a lot of negative people, I don't think that way. I'm an optimist. I'm the kind of guy who would go after Moby Dick in a row boat and take the tartar sauce with me! I believe the glass is half full, not half empty.

Every day I practiced what to say and how to say it. People in my family laughed at me when I practiced my presentation in front of the mirror. It hurt my feelings, but I continued to do it.

The first day I went out to try to sell insurance, I threw up. That's how scared I was, but I still went out knocking on doors down on highway 69 in Kentucky.

I had one suit which I had bought using my mom's JC Penney's credit card. I'm thankful she let me do that. At the end of the first week, I had broken the company sales record by selling the most that had ever been sold in a week by any new agent or by any person in the company.

At the end of two years, I had a closing ratio of 1 out of every 2.6 people. The national average was 1 in 5. I currently have an agent working for me that holds the record for most ever sold for a career and over the last six years he's the highest salesman in the nation in our company.

I've made a multiple six figure income now for over 25 years in the insurance industry which I've been in for 38 years. I started out selling cancer policies door-to-door, so believe me I know something about hard work and perseverance.

Do I have a lot of things going against me? Yes, I do.

I was sexually molested as a child. Let's get real here. We're all two steps from insanity. There is not one of us as together as we act. None of us. None of us are as positive and happy as we act. We're all battling our demons, we're all have a trials, troubles and tribulations. So, if you get real and understand that everybody who is prosperous out there; sports, athletes or in the boardroom, every one of them are battling something. You must be like a duck and let water and messes roll off your back. If you don't, you'll spend your life in misery and there is just no sense in it.

Did you know there's more wealth in America today than there was on the entire planet in 1920? This a wonderful, prosperous time. If there ever was a time to believe in yourself and invest in yourself and your future, it is today.

But a lot of you can't believe. Your filter is negative. You're just too negative. You would demand a bacterium count on the milk of human kindness. Did you know there's never been a statue erected to a critic? You've got to rise above it.

This is how successful people succeed when other people don't. Some people believe the system is rigged against them or think you must have been born with a silver spoon or must have a great education. If you read my resume there wouldn't be anything very impressive there. But the truth is I make more money than most of the people who read my resume.

I like to work, I like to make money and I like to do good stuff with it. I've got 10 grandkids and I like to be generous to them. I like to give to charities. That's what I enjoy doing. Therefore, my success is not based on anything special about me, it's based on having a mindset to work and mindset to believe.

You need to understand that the biggest helping hand you will ever have is at the end of your own sleeve. If it's to be, it's up to me.

You need to understand that you might be your own problem. You need to look at yourself and if you're caught in a negative mindset, you can change. Nobody is stuck with who they are. Learn to be optimistic and believe things can work out for you.

My wife loves to shop. I always told my wife, "If we could ever find a job for you where all you needed to do was shop all day, we would be a massive success!"

We did find that job. She's our number one shopper in our multiple seven figure Amazon business.

We saw a Facebook video about Amazon FBA selling, and both were very interested. We like to work. We just think it's fun. Truthfully, I'd rather work and make money than just about anything. I fish, I've golfed, but I just think this is way more fun. We like to work, make money, and give it away.

We shut the television off for six weeks and consumed everything we could find about selling on Amazon.

We learned that FBA meant Amazon would ship the product to the customer and take care of customer service so we didn't have to. We learned that there were products in nearly every retail store we could think of that could be turned around and sold on Amazon for a profit, which is called arbitrage. We learned we could do it in brick and mortar stores and through their websites. As Gaye Lisby says, "There's money all around us."

After our first 12 months in the business we netted over $100,000, after all our expenses. That didn't shock me. I kind of anticipated that if we could keep up our buying that would happen. Remember this - the math doesn't lie. I'll come back to that in a little bit.

We joined a paid Facebook group of like-minded people and we loved it. The information there went far beyond the free information available in other groups and on You Tube. In addition, we felt like we were in a group of caring people who could help us avoid newbie mistakes which brings me to my very first tip.

TIP #1
INVEST IN COACHING GROUPS

Sign up to work with qualified and honest coaches, not some guru trying to make a name for himself. Remember, you don't know what you don't know.

Almost immediately after joining the paid Facebook group, we signed up for the small group coaching that was available.

Since that time, I try to attend the masterminds and soak up anything I can from other sellers. I continue to invest in coaching groups, which really is an investment in myself and my business growth.

Earlier this year, I was in another mastermind that was $6,000 to join and $500 a month continuing forward. Some sellers make the mistake of saying they can't afford to join coaching groups or masterminds. I understand, and I respect that highly, but let me throw this out as a form of encouragement. I personally have never been to college, and yet I've made a six-figure income for 25 years.

I've been in the insurance business for 38 years and I've coached and trained people all over the nation. I've got people who work for me now that make six-figure plus incomes and have for many years who I personally trained to do so.

There's nothing special about me. I'm as average as cornbread which you could tell if you heard my southern accent, but I had been around, and I've worked, and I've met a lot of very, very successful people. I found a lot of them are really common, in fact, a lot more common than one may think.

The dean of Case Western Reserve University, Richard Osborne, was one of the most successful people I've ever met. He was a billionaire. I got to know Richard while I was very young, and Richard helped me to understand a lot about business and I'm eternally grateful to him for that. He's gone now, but he invested himself in me and I invested in learning everything I could from him.

I'm amazed how many will spend tens of thousands for a college degree and won't make much money. Then when they come on something like this, they won't spend $2,900 to join a program to really learn.

It's those people who don't understand the law of the harvest. They don't understand sowing and reaping. You've got to sow before you reap.

Become Humble. Become a student. Invest in coaching groups. I've done it and encourage you to do it too. Don't skip this step.

Tip #2

To Sell a Lot You Must Buy a Lot

Let me tell you a little something that will change your life.

First off, I'm not a minister, but I do love the Lord. Apostle Paul said he was a chief sinner, but I hadn't been born yet so I guarantee I've sinned far more he has. But I want to read something to you. It's biblical, but it's not meant to be something to bother anybody that does not have faith or does not honor faith. I wouldn't do that for anything. But at the same time, this is where my teaching came from.

I was raised by a wonderful father and mother, but my dad was poor and worked all the time. I learned a lot about business from my dad: the right way and the wrong way.

My dad truck patched a lot and he worked at a factory. (Truck patching is when you sell the vegetables grown in your garden from your pick-up truck on the side of the road.)

He would often quote this to us. Please listen to this, because I want to teach you a little bit about business by using a Bible verse because I'm more interested in your psychology than I am teaching you all the tools about how you scan for products or things of this nature.

So, listen to this. This was written by a man that is often written down in history as being the wisest man who ever lived, Solomon, written in Ecclesiastes. Listen to this and then I'm going to explain it. "He, that observeth the wind shall not sow and he that regardeth the clouds shall not reap."

Let's take that word wind, he that observeth the wind of fear and regardeth of the clouds of doubt shall not reap. Fear and doubt are thoughts that cripple all of us, including me. I raise my hand first.

Smart People Have Courage to Ask Dumb Questions

Rebekah Hawkins Ok, here's mine. I was looking around to see if there was a spreadsheet on how to figure out the numbers. So, if I want to make X dollars per month then I should be sourcing and spending X dollars per week. Or something like that. Surely there is a formula to figure out how to reach your end goal, right?

Garry L. Ray After my first 2 years in the business and we had sold over 1.2 Million I ran the numbers and it equated to a 2.24 multiplier. Meaning for every dollar I spent it translated into $2.24 in sales. 10,000 = 22,400 in sales. so to sell 1 Million a year you need to buy 1900 a day 5 days a week as a close rough number.

 Garry L. Ray

🛡 Admin · December 11 at 8:33 PM

What is your next big mistake you will make as a newer seller on Amazon? It most likely will be thinking that sales stop after Q4. It is almost funny for veteran sellers because we know that the WORLDS largest retailer (larger than WM) Amazon, sells year round.

If you stop sourcing and buying because Q4 is over you make an error in judgement. If you RA, keep it up. If you OA (Online Arbitrage) keep it up. If you subscribe to list (I have 8) cancel them at your own defeat.

Yes refine your buying some to back to normal, but we have made some big bucks sourcing and selling in Q1.

We are having the best Q4 ever, but we will keep buying and selling and making money in Jan-March as always.

Your next biggest mistake just might be forgetting that there is money to be made sourcing and selling after Christmas. Remember the Worlds largest platform never ever stops selling, and they need you to source and ship. Perhaps better said You need You to source and ship!

The only way to conquer fear and doubt is you act as though you don't have fear and you act as though you don't have doubt. How would the person who does not have fear act? How would he operate in the Amazon business? Well, a person that doesn't have fear would buy product. A person who does not have doubt, would buy product.

You may have fear and you may have doubt, but don't act with fear and don't act with doubt. Act with confidence, act secure, act like "I know what I'm doing," and when you do that, you will get success and you'll get results even though inside you may have fear and you may have doubt.

Now that applies to me and that applies to you. It applies to every one of us in any business venture because I've been in other businesses too. I know that applies to everything. You cannot let yourself get all bound up by fear and by doubt. If you do that and you act like fear and you act like doubt, you will not succeed. You cannot let it cripple you.

This truth is critical so let me share one written by the Apostle Paul. He said, "But this I say, he who would sow sparingly, shall also reap sparingly, and he who would sow bountifully, shall reap also bountifully."

Common sense, right? A person who sows one acre of corn, will get an acre of results. The person who sows 1000 acres will get 1,000. Is it really that simple? Yes, it is. It really is that simple. And the over-complication of this simplicity is what binds people up. Some things are just so simple, they do not need to be bound up.

You must sow to reap, you must conquer your fear and your doubt and the only way to conquer fear and doubt is

There is no hope for someone who scoffs at optimism. Optimism is magical. Those who use it are often thought of as being more intelligent than they are, luckier than they are and those who use optimism as a carpenter uses a hammer, will be the envy of those who depend on circumstances and talent.

with some success and the only way to have that success is to act unafraid and act like you do not have doubt.

To sell a lot, you must buy a lot. And, to pull the trigger on the kind of buys you need to be making, you have to get rid of doubt. Look at the numbers and remember the math doesn't lie. Don't overthink it. Don't freeze up. Don't fall to fear and doubt.

You can't sell what you don't have and you won't have anything if you're bound up by fear and doubt.

Confront it. Get rid of it. You have a business to build.

Tip #3
Use a Repricer

Here's the thing about a repricer- a lot of people focus on the repricer as being able to drop the prices to compete for the Amazon Buy Box. That's totally true, but they get afraid and think their margins are going to disappear.

However, here's the other thing it does, it can take your price up. I have had prices jump within seconds because other third-party sellers sell out, and boom, the price will jump and that's the beauty of a repricer.

Here's the other thing though about a repricer. The repricer keeps you from looking at your products all the time. You only have so many hours in a day.

You start off every day at a 100 percent energy level and end at about 30 and 40, but and as I've understood this, anytime you drop below 50 percent in your energy level, you're entering a negative energy zone. And when you enter a negative energy zone, you increase the odds of making bad decisions, hurting people's feelings, being mean to your wife, being rough to your husband, being hateful with your children.

You should always be careful if you sense that you're getting close to that negative energy zone.
You might need to shut everything down, walk away, take a nap, do something because you do not want to hurt people you love. You can hurt your spouse and it can take years to fix that.

I recently did that. I was in a negative energy zone and I recently hurt somebody's feelings. I didn't mean to do that for anything, but it all happened because I was in a negative energy zone. I wished I could change it. I apologized and that's what we all need to do. Negative energy zones affect everyone else.

A good repricer keeps you from getting into that negative energy zone because you're not sitting around at 10:00 at night going, "Why haven't I sold any of these?" Then you look, and you see that the price has dropped $4 and you're thinking, "but I wouldn't mind dropping it $4 if I could sell them, I need my money back."

All along a repricer would've sold it for you when it dropped ten cents, thirty cents, or a dollar. You didn't sell then. You wouldn't have lost that $4 that you're now willing to lose just to move the product at 10:00 at night!

A new seller recently asked me how many items a person should have in their inventory before they think of getting a repricer. That's the wrong question. I think the correct question is how big do I want to get?

You could be starting off with five products. If my coach tells me to get a repricer I'm getting a repricer because next week I'm going to have 20 products and next month 200. I think probably the better question is how big do you want to get?

The repricer will also help you to go ahead and roll your product, sell it, get your money back, and buy more. But the only way to buy more, is you've got to sell out what you've got.

Keep your money in motion

I see sellers just toiling, toiling, and wasting so much energy over this $5 loser. I don't mean to be rude; maybe I say things too harsh, too strong and I'm sorry for that, but I want to tell you, you're thinking so small minded when you do that. This isn't softball, this is baseball and the pitches are coming hard and fast. You must dig those cleats in, focus and you've got to bust that ball.

The only way to do this is to put product in, sell it, get your money, hopefully a profit, and roll on into the next product buy.

Get a repricer and you will have fewer losers because as the market is going down it will lower your prices, keeping you at or near the Buy Box, so you sell it before all profit is totally gone. Making 2% as a product's value is collapsing is better than losing 50%.

I would like to share some new information I have learned, but kind of afraid I might not teach it well.

I have done an experiment and discovered that if your item has a price that is way above the buy box price, your item is more likely to be placed into Fulfillment Center (FC) transfer, than an item which is close to or at the buy box at the time of receiving at Amazon.

Example. You paid $20 for an item. At the time you entered it into Inventory Lab or directly into your seller account, that item was selling for $120. So obviously you matched the buy box for $120. You then set your repricer to let it potentially fall all the way down to $40 at your minimum.

You then think you can walk off and your repricer will take care of lowering the price if the market tanks. But here is what I have discovered.

If your item is a hot item and flying off the shelf of Amazon's warehouse but the price has fallen from the original price you entered, when the assembly line takes the products out of the box and scans the bar code, they can't see that you intend for your repricer to lower it.

Your item may then be placed into FC transfer if Amazon needs products in another part of the nation. It then can take 2 to 7 days for your product to go live and sell.

The bottom line is your repricer will not adjust the price of your item until it goes live. It can be and in many cases is, placed into FC transfer because your sell price was so high.

The remedy for this is to check your hot selling items daily before the shipments arrive and lower your set price for the item just in case you want it to go ahead and sell at that $40 level or so.

Yes, we all want to make the big profits, but it is the base hits that always wins the game.

Having and correctly managing a repricer is absolutely a must.

Tip #4
Learn to Lose Money to Make Money

I'll give you an example of this idea: this past January and February, my wife and I had a loss in our Amazon account, intentionally.

I knew how much money we had made through the year before and I knew how much I thought I was going to make this year. I told her, "Let's liquidate." The reason why I liquidated is because November and December last year had been so profitable for us, I could still liquidate those slow movers, that dead inventory, at a loss and come out way ahead.

It was time to refresh our inventory. We use Informed.com for our repricer. We have a setting in there called Liquidate. Liquidate is match the buy box all the way down. We're going to own the buy box. We're going to own it all the way down to some really low figure and get it cleared out. I click liquidate and that item's going to get out the door. So instead of making 15 or 20 bucks, I'll make $6 or $7, but it's out the door. I don't have to think about it anymore.

That's how to lose money in order to make money. It's hard for people to understand, but it is absolutely essential.

Years ago, I was raising Angus cattle. I had 100 head of black Angus cattle, but I had this one cow that every year her calf would get sick. When a calf gets pneumonia, it's going to spread it to the others. The first year that happened, I just thought it was a fluke. I doctored the calf, I quarantined the calf and cow and sure enough some of the other calves got it and died. Suddenly, I'm losing money. The second year she had a calf again and the same thing happened. So immediately when that happened, that cow and calf got loaded in the trailer, and taken to the sale barn. They were off my property.

I took it to the market, sold it, lost tons of money because she wasn't worth a dime and the calf had pneumonia, but she had to go.

You cannot let losers stay around, because they pull your attitude down. It gets you depressed if you worry over that one item and the lost money. You can't do that.

I bought a large wholesale buy from a guy I met in Las Vegas. We had lunch together one day and hashed out a deal and he told me something that I realized immediately was smart.

As he makes his buys, he creates an MSKU that reflects that buy. Once he's made the percentage of profit he's after on that entire buy, he liquidates the rest. He thinks, "I've made my profit, nobody can take that profit away from me." If he buys a huge buy of Macy's bedding, like 15 to 20 stores, he puts $80,000 or whatever into that buy. Once he gets his 20 percent back, he liquidates the rest of it. That is so brilliant.

You can do it monthly. You can go back and say, here's all my buys for the month of May. I've made money. I've done well. I'm liquidating the rest of it. You've got to learn to get rid of your losers even if it means taking a loss on those units. Don't get hung up on losses on individual items.

Here's another thought- what if you pulled up all the buys you made for this past July? Say you bought 250 individual products? You've invested into 250 ASINs for that month. What if you review the entire monthly investment (buys) and you see that you spent $10,000 for the month of July on these ASINs?

Let's say you now see that of the 10,000 you invested, your sales on the 250 buys is already at $2,100 profit? That means you already have made back all your investment ($10,000) and made $2,100 extra. This means you made 21% on the $10,000 invested, correct?

Now watch this! You're now managing the losers. It is stressing you, you're constantly feeling like you messed up, because you have 17 of the 250 that are big losers? Or are they?

If you are an amateur you think you have lost, but a pro will put those into the whole large basket and realize that he/she has already made a fantastic 21% on the entire monthly buys including these losing 17 skus.

Dump them! Yes, dump them! Match the buy box and liquidate and get the remaining money back into your hands to buy hot products with. And remember the month of July was very profitable. Cash out and reinvest. That's what I mean by don't be afraid to lose money to make money.

Tip #5
Learn the Difference Between Nickle Work Versus Dollar Work

To be a success as an Amazon seller, the number one job you must do well is buy product. Nickle work is the prepping, shipping, paperwork and there's a certain amount of that you must do when you start out. But dollar work is buying. That's where the real money is.

Consider this: we were averaging about $30,000 a month when we realized we needed help.

We reached out to a neighbor of ours who had four children and while they were in school, we trained her to prep, ship, and enter things into Inventory Lab for us. This one decision caused us to able to expand.

We started her off at $10 an hour, but very quickly moved her to $12 an hour. People said, "How can you afford to pay her?"

I had done the math. I knew all we needed to do was sell an additional $10,000 per month and that would pay her salary. With an additional $10,000 in sales a month, we wouldn't have to prep/ship, a neighbor gets a great job and gets to be there for her kids after school. It was a win-win.

But notice what happened to us!

We jumped from $30,000 per month in sales to $60,000 per month in sales in only about 40 days.

It only cost us $10,000 in sales to pay her per month, so we profited over $20,000 per month just by making that addition.

I'm blown away by people who can't grasp living with an open hand. We could have said, "We need to keep all that for ourselves." If we had been like that, we would never have been able to scale up.

You're making money in this business by buying. That's number one. We were in San Diego sitting around a big boardroom table. Gaye Lisby was on the other side of the table. We were listening to each one talk about business aspects, building systems and so on. After a time, she spoke up and made one of the biggest, boldest comments that left people talking about it for a long time.

She said, "All of us should remember this: we're in the business of buying." Then she paused for dramatic effect.

So true! As an Amazon seller we're all doing 100 things but buying is number one. If we're not buying, we're not doing what really makes the money.

We must delegate as much nickel work as we can, so we can focus on the dollar work of buying. As I speak about hiring somebody to do this kind of work, I know some of you think you can hardly afford to hire somebody.

I totally respect that you'll have to work your way into it. All you really need to do is to be able to float a person's paycheck for about three weeks and you will be able to buy, get enough in, ship it out and sell it, and from that point on, that person will pay their own paycheck.

I want to talk to you a little bit again about your psychology, about your psyche. If you've trained a lot of people, coached a lot of people like I have you learn about something that blocks what we're trying to do.

Let me explain what it is. If you're a person that is prone to jealousy, you're going to restrict your ability to be successful at very much of anything. You need to clearly understand that a person who is jealous sees the worst in everything they see. They see a rose and instead of loving the fragrance, they negative about all the little jagged rough edges.

People who are jealous look at me and say, "If I made the money they made, I'd have a good attitude, too."

Years ago, I used to teach a self-help class where my boss would pay for our employees to come and spend a week. For a week I would train these people using the Zig Ziglar material. I would train these people on these different steps to become successful - attitude, hard work, desire, all that stuff, but I learned something going through that. I sent a woman home one time. I wouldn't let her stay for the week. She was too cynical.

Happiness is found when you stop trying to compare yourself to other people.

I mean this woman was cynical and everything we tried to teach her about happiness, success, being positive with whatever, she would shoot down. Finally, on Wednesday morning I dismissed her and let her go. Her boss fired her about a month later because he said he got fed up with it too.

My point is, you can't let red ants destroy your business. You cannot let controversial mindsets and people that are cynical, negative and so on destroy what you're doing..

Even as you read my words, you must filter me out to listen to the message. Never, ever, ever lose sight of a message just because there's something that irritates you about the messenger. And realize that jealousy is a vile poison that will stop your business from succeeding and stop you from succeeding.

Quick, true story. Biblical story. King David is out on his balcony, he looks down, he sees a woman bathing down here.

We all know the story. He wants that woman. He decides he's going to take that woman but finds out the woman is married. "I've got to get rid of the husband." He gets the husband, sends him out to war on the front line. Man goes to the frontline, man gets killed. King David gets a guy killed in order to steal his wife.

King David was the only person in the whole bible history that was ever said to be a man after God's own heart, only one, but he did something horrible.

Here's what happened. There is a prophet named Nathan who comes to David and says to him, "A rich man had these vineyards and all this wealth, flocks of sheep and cattle, and is a very wealthy man. He sees a poor man who only has one little sheep, one he carried around and raised up from a little lamb. The rich man comes in and takes the very thing the poor man loved so dearly. What should be done to him?"

King David said, "That man should be put to death."

Nathan looks him dead in the eye and says, "You are that man."

Now the bible says immediately King David started the process of repentance.

He became jealous of another man over his wife so much so that he committed murder to have her, but when he was confronted with the truth, he repented.

If you're suffering from jealousy, it will block your ability to learn from others and increase your earnings. It just does.

If someone else has success, make a friend of them, find out what they're doing so you can learn to do it too. Lay down jealously and let it go.

Jealousy will limit your ability to learn from the very people that you need to learn from, perhaps someone that's truly smarter. When you're confronted with somebody that's smarter, drop your ego. Learn to be a student. Drop the ego. Humble yourself.

Learn the difference between nickel work and dollar work and get rid of jealousy so you can learn to be the very best buyer you can be.

The best helping hand you'll ever have is at the end of your own sleeve.

Tip #6
You Have the Same Thing as all Billionaires

Stop wasting time.

People say they don't have time to learn, don't have time to change their lives, but will sit down in front of TV and waste hours without a thought between they're ears. In the meantime, the billionaire is reading, working, studying, finding ways to improve his bottom line.

When we started in the Amazon business, we turned off the TV and went through video after video. We consumed all the information we could.

We only allowed ourselves Sundays to worship, rest, and get together with friends.

You must understand that if you say you really want to change your life, build your business, or learn something new, you can do it. You just might not choose to do it. If that's the case, then quit being envious of people who have money because people who have money swapped something for that money.

Garry L. Ray
⊙ Admin · July 17

I am your constant companion.
I am your greatest asset or heaviest burden.
I will push you up to success or down to disappointment.
I am at your command.
Half the things you do might just as well be turned over to me.
For I can do them quickly, correctly, and profitably.
I am easily managed; just be firm with me.
Those who are great, I have made great.
Those who are failures, I have made failures.
I am not a machine, though I work with the precision of a machine and the intelligence of a person.
You can run me for profit, or you can run me for ruin.
Show me how you want it done. Educate me. Train me.
Lead me. Reward me.
And I will then...do it automatically.
I am your servant.
Who am I?
I am a habit

Be effective with your time and don't waste it. You have the same 24 hours anyone else has.

Tip Number Seven
Stay Shallow and Wide

Go deep only when you know your stuff. If you're new in this business, stay shallow and wide, by buying only two to four of any items until you're in the business for at least six months.

We studied the Keepa charts of product sales histories. We looked for trends in pricing.

We learned that if we bought in the top 1% of the best seller's rank (BSR) that product was going to sell. If we scanned it or sourced it either in store or from an online arbitrage list and found it was profitable at 30% or more, we pulled the trigger.

Remember, math does not lie.

Garry L. Ray
🛡 Admin · October 10, 2017

This is so simple I wonder if I should even post it. But to help the new members and give back for all I have received from my good friend Gaye Lisby, here is a very simple money making tip.

When scanning at Walmart, make sure to use the WalMart app on your phone. There is a little barcode scanner button in the upper right hand of the screen. press it and scan the barcode of any item and it will give you the price in that store for that item.

Close to 25% of the "Clearance" items we source at WM will have a lower price than what is stickered. Recently Kimberly Jordan Ray bought about $800 at one WM and over half she would have missed had she not used the WM app.

When you check out make sure the register price is what you scanned, if not scan it right there in front of them and they will charge what is on your screen.

This is truly a money making tip, I promise!

Also carry an ink pen and when you WM scan and get that lower price write it on the sticker real small so when you check out you will know what it should ring up for, I have too bcse my memory is so bad lol.

All my best to everyone, we are looking forward to closing out our 2 Million in sales by the end of Jan and have only been doing this for 27 mths as of now. It works, if you do!

"Learn the tools, then develop the art".

Many of you are watching Gaye and you think she makes it look easy, that is because she has developed the "art". People who are successful at anything make it look easy. Thats because they learned the tools of their trade then developed the art. "Learn all the tools, then develop the art".

Love you all,,

Stay shallow and wide, go deep only when you know your stuff. A lot of new people go too deep, too quickly on an ASIN and get burned when a price drops.

We still stay shallow and wide, but now we can read the signals better and know when to buy a dozen here and a dozen there, or much more.

Our success has been intentional. Realize that success leaves clues and success is duplicatable.

Tip #8
Invest in Paid Lists

We subscribe to every good online arbitrage list we find. From the beginning, I knew these lists would work if I could learn how to work a list.

See how that is opposite of the way some people think?

Some people are so cynical, so infected, they've got to be negative. If it is a nice day with a beautiful breeze, they've got to say, "Yes, but a storm's probably coming."

You can't be like that and sow the good seeds that create a great harvest in your business. You've got to learn how to keep a positive mindset.

We order from 8 online arbitrage lists and have trained a young lady who now does it for us.

We take every ASIN we see and make a daily habit of trying to add it to our inventory, even if we're not really going to sell it, just so we can get unrestricted if Amazon has listing limitations on it.

Here's the invisible thing that happens behind the scene. One of these days, you're going to drop an ASIN in there and that ASIN is going to free you up on 10, 20 other ASINs the next time you drop them in. Because Amazon has this algorithm and certain ASINs trigger other ASINs.

Some of you wonder why some of us can sell so much stuff? Well, we've been doing this for years and I still do. I still drop ASINs in all the time because I know they trigger others for auto-approval.

I cannot believe people who ask me for advice, then I'll recommend an OA list then six months later find out they're not on the list anymore. I'm making money off the exact same list in the exact same places they said the money wasn't there.

They don't have the same logic I have about lists and it's very simple. If I pay 150 bucks a month for a list, I'm not expecting to make $49,000 off it. If I'm paying $150, I need to make $151. If I make $151, the list pays for itself. But some of the lists I have, I'm making as much as 10 to 15 times what I'm paying for the list.

Learn the tools-Master the art

I keep track of all the buys, so I know. They're all profitable for me. We have a google sheet and every time we buy something, we note what list that comes from. I'm telling you from experience, I can sort that thing and know if I'm making money on those lists. I'm making money on every list we've got.

Some people say, "I can't. I can't do these lists because I'm not ungated in those brands and categories." You're not going to get ungated unless you get these lists and you start dropping them into Seller Central's add a product line and clicking to get listing limitations lifted.

You must pay a tuition in order to graduate. You know you must pay the toll if you want to drive on this highway of success and the toll is money and time, money and time. You've got to spend money and you've got to invest time and if you do that, you will make money doing this.

Even if you're only going to be sourcing in-store rather than on-line, paid lists can be valuable and put you onto profitable products which you can then pick up in the store.

We tried learning tools like Tactical Arbitrage, but I do not have the time to sit around and filter through all those leads, weed out the mismatches, find the profitable ones, see if they can be ordered. There can be thousands of pieces of data, and I'm not going to do that when it's already done for me by buying off a list.

I respect those who want to hire their own virtual assistants to do that for them. That's just fine. For me, the fewer people I have to supervise the happier I am.

I like the fact the young lady who works for us makes our online buys for us every day, just like clockwork, and I can go on to something else.

I like to drive. That's why I love to do retail arbitrage too. All that scenery passing is just like a movie. I love it.

I also like the knowledge that I've given myself several exit strategies. For example, if the products in retail stores dried up for me, I know I've got online arbitrage. If my private label products all of the sudden tanked, I've still got several ways to go.

A smart business person gives themselves several options. Buying from lists is just one of them for us, put it is a very profitable option.

Garry L. Ray

⛊ Admin · December 11 at 9:26 PM

Why keep a secret among friends? Look at the picture of just one buy we made off of Gaye's list.

This picture will show only 1 ASIN.

Again I repeat this is only 1 buy we made from dozens and dozens of buys, these list over time are GOLD! But that's my opinion, oh yeah and Inventory Lab's proof, very profitable indeed! Look and then multiply by many many buys.

This one ASIN we ordered at different times from the same merchant and have made 11 sales of just this one ASIN.

Oh yeah get this 100.80% ROI, on these 11 sales of this 1 ASIN

The ASIN is in the picture, so I am hiding nothing.

Garry Ray

Tip #9
Hire Help

Did you know success is also scalable?

Some Amazon sellers want to grow, but they come to Number Nine and they just won't take the step. At the risk of sounding overly simplistic, what's happening is you're focusing too much on the glass half empty and not half full. Once you've made your money, don't be greedy, don't wear yourself out trying to do every step in your business.

You need to be buying product. Maybe that means you go out sourcing in the stores more. That means, once you get your list buying criteria set, out-source that to someone else and let them do the buying for you.

Don't be so greedy. Let loose of some of your money and hire some people. They'll make you money, but you're also helping somebody else's life. You're not necessarily just spending money to make money. You're also making somebody else's life better. We were learning the difference between nickel work and dollar work when we hired that lady to ship for us. Our sales went up because we could spend more time buying.

But something else happened as well. We trained her, and she started doing so well in the business, she could escalate and now she's running her own prep center, doing a great job for other sellers.

The lady we've hired now to do our ordering is a stay-at-home mom with a small child. She doesn't want to put the child in daycare. She's loving this. So, we've helped her life. Her life's better. She's making us money. She's making money for herself. It's a win-win. Try to be a good person and understand hiring people is another way of spreading the wealth around.

As important as your past is, what is more important is your future.

Most of what causes or kills success is attitude. And most of what hinders a good attitude is past events.

The more you feel sorry for yourself, the worse you will feel. The more you justify yourself in your own "self-talk" that you have a right to feel sorry for yourself, the farther your boat is floating from the shoreline of happiness.

Here is a simple psychological test to help predict your future. Choose one and be honest:
"I consider myself to be a lucky person."
"I consider myself to be an unlucky person."

No babbling about there is no such thing as luck, that isn't the point of the exercise. The point is people who see themselves as lucky or blessed are psychologically happier, live longer and are more successful than those who believe that for the most part bad things happen to them more than good things do- that they are "unlucky."

I stumbled onto this about 35 years ago and it literally changed my life. Up until then I had trained myself to believe that, "if it weren't for bad luck, I'd have no luck at all. Gloom despair and agony on me."

When I caught that my future was going to be strained because for the most part, I was unlucky, it scared me as a 21-year-old. I went to work to change my thinking, to believe that good things are going to happen to me.

Taurin Bellavance shared a link.
December 10 at 12:29 PM

I just finished watching this video Garry L. Ray did in March with Gaye Lisby. A year or two ago it wouldn't have affected me much. I default to cynicism and negativity and it took me a long time to get by all of that but I can 100% say it's the reason that I've grown so much this year. This stuff is big. I have never gotten anything out of motivational speakers but something to scoff at, but I also let fear and doubt guide a lot of my decisions in this business and watched friends do very well on products and strategies that I said no to. I used to get upset about returns, OA inventory arriving damaged, getting stuck with inventory that I had to take a slight loss or break even on. No more. There's a lot of fear out there around the what-ifs when we're selling on Amazon - suspensions, product not selling, IP complaints, etc. They're all things to be prepared for and wise about, but if not kept in check that fear will absolutely hold you back.

i

YOUTUBE.COM

Garry Ray with Gaye Lisby, Blasting Doubts and Blowing up Sales Records

Here's the replay on Blasting Doubts and Blowing up Sales Records with Multiple- 7 Figure Amazon...

If you're reading this and think this is bunk, that your outlook on luck either way cannot influence your life, then you are sunk. It is a law of attraction- like a magnet.

How you view yourself lucky/unlucky, blessed/punished will determine your future. As the Bible says (yes it says this), "For as a man thinks in his heart so is he."

Translated: think bad, gloom, doom - get it. Think happy, prosperous, fortunate - get it.

Some people live a life of woe, some live a life of happiness. Those who live a life of woe, are constantly living in despair. Why doom yourself?

Change.

I did.

You can too.

Some folks might say I have an over-simplistic view of Amazon selling. I don't think I do.

Most people aren't in this to win guru status. They're just trying to make a better life for their family.

Most Amazon third party sellers are common folks just like you and me. They know the value of a dollar. They work hard for their time and money. They just need a little clearer vision on some things.

I believe if you will take to heart the things in this book, you too can find Amazon arbitrage success. I know we have and I know hundreds, perhaps thousands who have to. These are people personally known to me. They're my friends.

If you're looking to add a six figure income to your life, or perhaps a multiple six figure income, I promise you can do it on Amazon.

I did, and continue to do so.

Smart People Have Courage to Ask Dumb Questions

Tracey Foster Young Do you still only buy in the top 1%? I keep that thought in my mind when sourcing since I heard you say that a couple of times. Do you do that as well with lists you get for OA, or is only for RA that you apply that?

Garry L. Ray Great question. Yes top 1% BUT my buyer for the list uses Jungle Scout Pro and if an item sells 30 a month or more, then we buy a few, so it could be perhaps top 2% but no OA under 30 sales a month. When RA just top 1%. UNLESS it is a huge profit item like a PC and the profit is say $100 or more, then we will go lower than top 1%. Long answer sorry.

Andrew Chang If I recall correctly, you get a 20% ROI after paying your employees. Does this mean if you want to make 10,000/month you will have to spend

50,000/month on items or $2500/day? And were you able to purchase that much from 8 lists or were you doing RA as well?

Garry L. Ray Andrew Chang YES ROI is Return On Investment (which you know I'm explaining for others.) In this scenario the $50,000 spent is the investment. 50,000 x 20% = $10,000. Also, we do online arbitrage from lists and retail arbitrage in stores also. RA is quicker income, while OA is best chance to get replenishable inventory. Just today our person who works our list bought $950 worth and I worked two stores while my wife worked two stores. Total bought today $4,400. Yesterday the OA buying = $2,950.

Andrew Chang What is your cut off on old inventory? 3 months? or do you start liquidating once you had enough on one Asin? When do you start liquidating Christmas items?

Garry L. Ray Andrew Chang Maximum of 5-6 months, then liquidate. Or, if it is a large group buy (those are few anymore) then as soon as that group hits 30% profit on the entire group buy, or 6 months whichever comes first we liquidate. My brother-in-law used to manage a huge hog operation for a wealthy farmer. He ran the numbers for years and discovered that after a brooder sow had her 7th litter of pigs, she started having fewer pigs, and having to eat more to maintain herself. This huge operation decided to sell all sows after the weaning of the 7th litter. The profit in this operation went up 40% (which is HUGE) by doing so. This is liquidation in another field but it's still a great example. They could sell the sow for a good profit and reinvest in a better animal which was more productive.

GLOSSARY OF TERMS

FBA: Fulfillment by Amazon, a service provided by Amazon to sellers that includes Amazon receiving the product, shipping the product to the customer and providing customer service on the transaction.

Arbitrage: buy products low and sell them at a profit

OA: online arbitrage, or buying from store sites online, and selling the products on Amazon.

RA: retail arbitrage, or buying in stores, and selling the products on Amazon.

Third Party Sellers: any seller who offers products on the Amazon platform that is NOT Amazon themselves.

BSR: Best Sellers Rank, a ranking system of how well certain products in certain categories sell on Amazon.

Scanning: the act of using the Amazon seller scanning app, or other phone apps to scan upc codes of products in store and comparing them to Amazon listings to find profitable products.

Source: any store, online, or brick-and-mortar where profitable products can legally, morally and ethically be sourced.

Prepping: the act of preparing a product according to Amazon's warehouse guidelines for shipment into Amazon's fulfillment centers.

SKUS: Stock Keeping Units: In the field of inventory management, a stock keeping unit is a distinct type of item for sale.

Want to learn more from Garry Ray?

Want your mindset to be crafted from gloom and agony to success and victory?

Coach Garry Ray does this for Amazon Third Party Sellers who are ready to massively increase their success in both life and business.

Join our secret Facebook group:

www.amazingfreedom.com/arbitrage

Garry and his lovely wife, Kimberly Jo, live in South Central KY near Bowling Green, KY.

They love and enjoy five grown children and ten grandchildren.

Garry entered the insurance business in March 1981, and still owns an agency of agents.

He and his marketing team have been responsible for 11 National Hall of Fame records.

Garry has been a public speaker and coach for the last 21 years.

He has owned three other businesses which he has since sold choosing to focus on the Insurance business and being the best Amazon third party seller he can be.

He and his wife stumbled onto the e-comm business 3 ½ years ago diving into OA and RA and loving it.

They have sold $2.5 million on Amazon featuring arbitrage and the private label products they recently developed.

They love to attend conferences and visited YIWU China in April 2018 to further their private label understanding.

While Kim's passion is her grandchildren, retail arbitrage, and piano practice, Garry's is his grandchildren and work, unless the University of Kentucky is playing basketball or a corvette needs to be driven, then you need to move, please. Now, if you don't mind.

Books Garry recommends:

Healing for Damaged Emotions, by David Seamands

Unlocking the Secrets to your Childhood Memories, by Kevin Lemand

Made in the USA
Coppell, TX
13 June 2021

57377059R00035